WHAT PEOPLE ARE SAYING ABOUT

ON THE UNHAPPINE~~ ~   REEK

A classic book ... a bitte.   ~wiedge ... it
examines with idiosyncratic   ..~ subject of Modern Greek
identity ... a truly patriotic book. Dimou places himself at the
right distance from his subject observing Greeks as they truly are.
Alexandros Stergiopoulos, Eleftherotypia Newspaper

Nikos Dimou had a different kind of unhappiness in mind when
he wrote *On the Unhappiness of Being Greek* back in 1975 ... yet all
the symptoms he described at the time contributed greatly
towards Greece's present predicament. The mentality that was
developed ... the national identity that was formed after the
military dictatorship ... we are still suffering from the same
symptoms and very soon we will find ourselves just as unhappy
(as we were back in 1975).
Chrystalla Chatzidimitriou, O Fileleftheros Newspaper

The 30th edition of *On the Unhappiness of Being Greek* has just come
out making this classic book a legend. There couldn't be a better
time for this new edition. I grew up with this book. In fact we
grew up together. I was a student when I first discovered it and
now I am what they call a middle-aged man. The only difference
between us is that, unlike myself, Nikos Dimou's book of
aphorisms – having gone against time and change – has remained
the same.

One cause for unhappiness for us Greeks is that this book has continued to be just as current as it was when it was first published ... another cause for unhappiness is the way the book was received back then ... especially by certain so called experts. They didn't see it as it really was (small bitter lessons for those who love Greece and maintain the irrational hope that somehow miraculously it will be saved) but as the exact opposite: a book that lays blame for no reason at all (all blame is unreasonable in Greece, it goes without saying). Along with those experts appeared the demagogues as well. These people never read books, they just argue about the books they never read. For all those good patriots this book was deemed to be dangerous. In the 90s ... everything that went against their attitudes, which were propagated in all the controlled media, was naturally labelled as 'dangerous'. It didn't help that Nikos Dimou was always in a peculiar black list ... because he had many flaws. First of all he was an advertising man and a successful one at that. Secondly, as his work has shown, he was never one to go with the flow of our nation's typical ideologies. On the contrary he fought against them as much as he could. Even worse, he never barricaded himself behind a particular caste, group, union or leftish ideology group so to be able to take part in the game. He remained the sensitive man that he was, who insisted on voicing his own opinions, (which is the reason why he did not last long in most newspapers and magazines he worked for.) ... I owe this man a lot and this is the least I can do to thank him for his poems, photographs, newspaper and magazine columns, the breath of fresh air he's been in our lives for so many years now. And rather unfortunately his remains the freshest voice in today's free presses.

So now that the banners of the fight have been ripped apart, now that the allure of the great expectations of those propagating

Greekness and anything Greek has worn off, the book has reappeared. And it is indispensable to us. *On the Unhappiness of Being Greek* has now become a classic best-seller and is again in the line of duty for a reason: it is high time young Greeks learned the reasons of our unhappiness so as to make their best in the coming decades to turn this book into a funny and bitter memory of all the lost years. I am happy this book has come out again. I am truly unhappy it remains so current.

www.eyelands.gr

On the Unhappiness of Being Greek was the title of one of Nikos Dimou's books that had caused a stir in the years following the military dictatorship. There was a line in the book: Whenever a Greek looks at himself in the mirror, he sees either Alexander the Great or Kolokotronis (hero of the Greek War of Independence) or (at least) Onassis. Never Karaghiozis (comic puppet character from the Greek popular shadow theatre.)

The truth of this observation has been corroborated many times in the past and it continues to be corroborated. For three consecutive decades, this country's indigenous residents have been refusing to accept that their participation in supranational organisations was not by way of compliment. They were not accepted in these organisations because of their nation's grandeur. It was an agreement with obligations for both sides: especially in the case of the European Union. … Our agreement with the European Union presupposes rights and obligations, too. We have claimed our rights. Our obligations have now prompted the creation of a fund. In today's Europe it is a misfortune to say that you are Greek.

George Lakopoulos, www.protagon.gr

On the Unhappiness of Being Greek

On the Unhappiness of Being Greek

Nikos Dimou

Winchester, UK
Washington, USA

First published by Zero Books, 2013
Zero Books is an imprint of John Hunt Publishing Ltd., Laurel House, Station Approach,
Alresford, Hants, SO24 9JH, UK
office1@jhpbooks.net
www.johnhuntpublishing.com
www.zero-books.net

For distributor details and how to order please visit the 'Ordering' section on our website.

Text copyright: Nikos Dimou 2012

ISBN: 978 1 78099 295 2

A CIP catalogue record for this book is available from the British Library.

Design: Stuart Davies

Printed and bound by CPI Group (UK) Ltd, Croydon, CR0 4YY

i

We operate a distinctive and ethical publishing philosophy in all
areas of our business, from our global network of authors to
production and worldwide distribution.

CONTENTS

In memory of Emmanuel Roides[1]

There are Greeks who question themselves and there are Greeks who don't. These reflections mostly concern the latter. They are dedicated, however, to the former.

N. D.

Introduction

On the Unhappiness of Being Human

1   We define happiness as the (usually temporary) state in which our desires coincide with reality.

2   Correspondingly, unhappiness must be the non-coincidence between desire and reality.

3   In other words, we could call unhappiness the gap between desire and reality.

4   The greater the gap, the unhappier we are.

5   Our happiness (or unhappiness) depends: on the magnitude, intensity and sum of our desires, on the one hand, and on the nature of reality, on the other.

6   I may be unhappy because I have excessive and inordinate desires that (quite rightly) remain unfulfilled. Or, then again, my desires may be 'reasonable' (moderate by human standards), but reality keeps dogging me (like Job). In this case we speak of ill-fortune.

7   We have a statistical sense of happiness. We think that a person with 'reasonable' desires should have an equal share of successes and disappointments.

(As proof: the expressions 'a change of luck', 'a turn of the wheel' etc.)

8   Life, however, does not confirm this view. Usually, those who have strong and numerous desires satisfy more of them than those whose desires are few and moderate. Except that the insatiable nature of the former rarely allows them to feel the state of equilibrium that we call happiness.

9   The gap that we called unhappiness functions both positively and negatively. I don't have what I desire, or I have something that I don't desire (e.g. an illness).

10 Those who offer 'recipes for happiness' usually try to modify or reduce desires – since it's not easy for them to alter reality. Naturally, the fewer desires we have, the less risk we run of being disappointed and hurt.

11 The next step is the doctrine of the Buddha, who teaches the suppression of desire as a foolproof antidote for unhappiness. (Even more effective: the negation of the source of all desire – the Ego.)

12 In animals, the gap between desire and reality is minimal. The basic pursuits of an animal are in keeping with the possibilities open to it. It is totally adapted to its surroundings.

13   It's difficult to talk of happy and unhappy animals –
     since the tension between these two (human) poles
     must not exist in them. Something tells me,
     however, that the birds of the air must be happy...

14   Unlike animals, man by convention and by nature
     has unfulfillable desires. He longs for immortality.
     Whereas the only thing he knows for certain about
     the future is that eventually he'll die.

15   We could define man as an animal that always
     desires more than it can attain. A maladjusted
     animal. In other words, we could define man as a
     being that carries unhappiness – innately – within
     it.

16   Or, then again, we could define man as a tragic
     animal. For what else is tragedy if not the agonized
     experience of the estrangement between man and
     the world?

17   The more human you are, in other words, the more
     you crave and seek, the wider the gap grows. And if
     you are a hero, you fight and lose. And if you are an
     artist, you try to fill the gap with forms.

18   If man, *qua* man, carries unhappiness within him,
     then certain categories of men have a greater predis-
     position for this. Even certain nations. And among
     these, for sure, are the Greeks. The modern Greeks.

19 The thesis of this book is that, due to history, heredity and character, the modern Greek reveals a wider gap between desire and reality than the average for other people.

20 So, if to be human already signifies the certainty of an amount of unhappiness – to be Greek portends a larger dose.

21 We can speak of 'the unhappiness of being Greek'.

On Greek Hyperbole

22 Axiom: a Greek does whatever he can in order to widen the gap between desire and reality.

23 He succeeds in this either by increasing his demands to an unreasonable degree, or by destroying his environment to the best of his ability. Or even by doing both.

24 The basic psychological factors in the widening of the gap: a permanent predisposition for hyperbole that always leads us to extremes and our – also permanent – inner inconsistency and inconstancy. Not for us the 'golden mean' of Aristotle.

25 A Greek lives cyclothymically – in a permanent state of elation or depression. As a consequence of which: a total incapacity for self-criticism and self-awareness.

26 'The nation must consider national whatever is true.'[2] For years now, we have been trying to convince ourselves of the opposite.

27 Whenever a Greek looks at himself in the mirror, he sees either Alexander the Great or Kolokotronis[3] or (at least) Onassis. Never Karaghiozis...[4]

28 And yet, in actual fact, he is Karaghiozis who imagines himself to be Alexander the Great. Karaghiozis with his many professions, his many faces, his constant hunger and his one skill: playacting.

29 How many Greeks (apart from Emmanuel Roides) have seen their real face in the mirror?

30 This is why the Greeks have never forgiven those 'anti-Greeks' who painted their portrait. (Poor About![5])

31 In all fields a Greek tries his hardest to be unrealistic. And then he is unhappy because he is unrealistic. (And then he is happy... because he is unhappy.)

32 Basically, Greeks are unaware of reality. They live twice above their financial means. They promise three times more than they can deliver. They claim to know four times more than what they actually learned. Their feelings (and emotions) are made to appear five times greater than what they actually feel.

33 Hyperbole is not just a national failing. It is a way of life for Greeks. It is the essence of their national identity. It is the basic cause of their unhappiness, but also their supreme glory. Because hyperbole in

self-awareness is known as *philotimo*.[6] Hyperbole in behavior is known as *leventia*.[7]

34   From the intentional or unintentional ignoring of reality, in its extreme forms, come tragedy and comedy. Both owe their existence to hyperbole and conflict.

35   Besides, the difference between tragedy and comedy is more a matter of perspective than content.

36   Neither the tragic nor the comic hero possesses any sense of measure, logic or humor.

37   There are various 'remedies' for reconciling the individual to reality. (The most sublime of these: religion. The most civilized: humor.) None of them works on a Greek. He lives (when he lives – and hasn't fallen into a state of lethargy) constantly in the gap between desire and reality. And when no gap exists – he provokes one.

38   A tragic way of life? Masochistic self-chastisement?

39   The modern Greek seems happy when he's unhappy. When everything is going well, he feels worried and uncomfortable. If he has no reason for being unhappy, he'll find one.

40   The happiness of the modern Greek's unhappiness is expressed perfectly by the Greek *grinia*[8] or grumbling.

41   A remnant of the Turkish yoke? A characteristic of afflicted peoples? Anyhow, the best that you'll hear is a deep (meaningful) sigh and the phrase: 'Well, you know, things could be better.'

42   For no other people on earth does the purely formal question 'How are you?' lead to a full analysis of the medical history, family circumstances, financial difficulties or sexual problems of the person asked.

43   The verbal masochism of the Greeks (as this is expressed in the modern Greek grumbling): inexhaustible, plethoric and monotonous.

44   There is a strange bond linking a Greek and his unhappiness. Which is why he is always at his best when he is unhappy or when he feels threatened. Crisis and conflict strengthen him. Negativity turns into positivity.

45   On the contrary, a Greek always finds a way of turning something positive into something negative. This might happen in a conversation (where the two people conversing suddenly change position for no other reason than to disagree), but also in any endeavor whatsoever (where immediately, as soon

as things are going well, the dissension starts).

46 For a Greek, negative is positive. So that when he has a position, he negates it in order to be able to begin again from negativity.

47 The Greek 'Parkinson's Law': two Greeks do in two hours (because of disagreement) what one Greek could do in one hour.

48 Present deep in the Greek soul are both Hadjiavatis[9] and Alexander the Great. Wretchedness and valor to a hyperbolic degree. The pride of hubris and the hubris of grumbling. Constant and ancient causes of unhappiness and creativity.

'N.I.C.' or Comparison in Time and Space

49   Any race believing itself to be descended from the ancient Greeks would be automatically unhappy. Unless it could either forget them or surpass them.

50   On the question of their heritage, I would separate the Greeks into three categories – the aware, the semi-aware and the unaware.

51   Those (very few) in the first category have first-hand knowledge. They have felt the awful burden of their heritage. They are aware of their ancestors' inhuman level of perfection in both word and form. And this crushes them.

52   ('I bore these stones for as long as I could endure.'[10])

53   The second category (the majority) do not have direct knowledge. But they've 'heard say'. They are like the sons of the famous philosopher, who are unable to understand his works, but see that those who do know them respect them and prize them. It bothers them, yet the fame flatters them. They always swell with pride – when talking to others.

54   It's terrible not only not to be able to surpass your father's work, but not to understand it either.

55 The more we pride ourselves on our ancestors (without knowing them), the more anxious we are about us.

56 The third category – the unaware – are chaste and pure (meaning uneducated: Makriyannis,[11] Theophilos,[12] simple folk). They've heard about the ancient Greeks in myths and legends that they have absorbed like popular folktales. It is these pure types who created the folk tradition and folk art. These alone lived without the anxiety of their heritage.

57 Nevertheless, it is the overwhelming majority of semi-aware, with their permanent hidden inferiority complex vis-à-vis the ancient Greeks, that determines the behavior and the attitude of the whole.

58 Victims not only of their heritage, but also of the most backward educational system in the world which views the ancient Greeks with such scholastic awe that it keeps them as glorious and as distant as possible.

59 (Or maybe there are other reasons for this so very wise system of ignorance concerning antiquity? A subconscious reaction, perhaps?)

60 Our relationship with the ancient Greeks is one of the sources of our national inferiority complex (N.I.C.). The other is the comparison in space rather than in time. With contemporary 'developed' peoples. With 'Europe'.

61 Whenever a Greek talks of 'Europe', he automatically excludes Greece. Whenever a foreigner talks of Europe, it's unthinkable for us that he should not include Greece.

62 So – just how European are we? There are many things separating us from Europe, perhaps more than there are uniting us. The major cultural movements which created modern European civilization had very little impact on us (with the exception of certain 'enlightened' minorities). Neither the Scholastic Middle Ages, nor the Renaissance, nor the Reformation, nor the Enlightenment, nor the Industrial Revolution. Perhaps, culturally speaking, we are closer to the Orthodox Russia of the Slavophiles than to the Europe of the Rationalists. And the Oriental influences?

63 It is a fact – whatever we may say – that we do not *feel* European. We feel 'outsiders'. And worst of all is that it bothers and rankles us so when we're told this...

64 We are envious of other peoples – though we proclaim our superiority. With a mania and an aversion for everything foreign, subservient and not only hospitable to (holidaying) foreigners.

65 At the root of Greek unhappiness are the two National Inferiority Complexes. The one in time – with the ancient Greeks. The other in space – with the 'Europeans'. Unjustified complexes perhaps – but no less real for that.

The Lost Face

66 We *are* different. Yet we desperately try to fit in somewhere. Why is it that we feel our uniqueness to be a failing? Why are we ashamed of it? Is it because we are not big enough or powerful enough to make a banner of our singularity? Or perhaps because we are not sure enough of ourselves?

67 (This lack of self-assurance – and not our size – always led us to seek 'guardians'. There are other small nations – but they don't allow themselves to become dependent on bigger ones...)

68 We never had any wish to clarify or understand our singularity. We were always doing our best to belong somewhere and not to be who *we are*. We tried to become the ancient Greeks again. We strove to prove the purity of our race, fanatically declaring war on every 'Fallmerayer'[13] to come along, but we never calmly investigated its actual characteristics. We disliked and destroyed our language because it didn't happen to be exactly the same as that of our ancient ancestors. We disliked ourselves because we weren't tall or fair and didn't have a 'Greek nose' like the Hermes of Praxiteles. We disliked our neighbors... because we resemble them. (The rage of Caliban seeing his own face in a glass?[14])

69 So who are we? The Europeans of the Orient or the Orientals of Europe? The developed people of the south or the underdeveloped people of the north? The (direct) descendants of the Achaeans or a Babel of motley races?

70 '... we renounced our country's traditions, yet we still do not share in the intellectual life of the nations of the west'.[15] Somewhere between the Zenith and the Nadir. Suspended. Like the tomb of Mohammed.

71 We are a people without a face. Without identity. Not because we don't have a face. But because we don't dare look at ourselves in the mirror. Because we've been made to feel ashamed of our real face. So much so that we are afraid to know ourselves. And so we learned to play different roles: that of the 'ancient Greek', that of the 'European'...

72 If the course of the Nation had been a little smoother, perhaps we wouldn't have had an identity problem today. Yet immediately after the end of centuries of subjugation, so many fell upon us – fighting to give us a new face – that we lost the face we had. Capodistrias,[16] the Bavarians,[17] the Philhellenes, the Erudite brought complete confusion to a people who had only just begun to absorb and strike a balance between the new cultural elements brought by the Europeans, Slavs,

Turks and Arvanites.[18]

73 Suddenly it seemed self-evident that the 'descendants of the ancient Greeks' couldn't *possibly* be Balkan peasants. And so everyone set about re-educating us. Against our will. And we had (it seems) an honest and warm face, like the writings of Makriyannis.

74 And so what for every people is self-evident, for us became a problem. (When you start thinking about your breathing, you lose its rhythm.)

75 How can a people without identity not have an inferiority complex... A people not allowed to be who they are, but who are always measured against other, foreign standards...

76 Somewhere deep down, the national complex (which was created for us) coincides with the Greek hyperbole. Hyperbole is a sign of someone who doesn't feel sure of himself. Someone who feels inferior. Hyperbole is an attempt to overcome this. Overcompensation.

77 Greeks will overcome the national complexes only when they find themselves. When they acquire identity and a face. When they stop hating themselves for what they are *not* and accept themselves for what they are.

78 If we don't find our own face soon, one day we are going to wake up with a 'general' face – a product of the roles we play, of fashion, of the media. Then we'll be left with a mask instead of a face. And the essence of Greekness will have been lost.

79 I don't know if what we need is national group therapy. What is needed, however, is self-knowledge, self-analysis and self-awareness. What's required is demythologization and, together with this, a new delineation. And above all, what's needed is a new form of education based on truth, which, amid all the make-up, will allow the real face of the race to emerge.

80 We often talk – more so lately – of freedom and independence. And what we mean is that the domestic oppression and external dependence on foreign powers has to stop. But we forget that oppression and dependence are rooted in our very selves. If the seeds weren't there inside us, no one would be able either to subjugate us or lead us on.

81 It's not the person who 'does what he wants' who is free, but the person who *knows* what he wants. As long as we don't know who we are, as long as we don't have a clear mind and a clear sense of responsibility, we will go from one form of dependence to the next.

82   Freedom does not only require 'virtue and boldness'.[19] Above all, it requires knowledge. And judgment.

83   But until we arrive at knowledge and maturity, the ailments of the Greek soul will provide the foundations for the unhappiness – and the glory – of the modern Greek.

84   For we mustn't forget: behind every creation is a wound of some sort. Inside every pearl is an irritating grain of sand.

Myths And Fears

85 A major symptom of the modern Greek soul: mythopoeia.

86 We fashion myths about ourselves. And then we are unhappy because we appear inferior to the myths (that we ourselves fashioned...).

87 One myth: 'A Greek's neck subjects itself to no yoke...'[20]

88 Try as I may, I'm unable to find any other people whose neck has been subjected to as many yokes as ours.

89 Except that here too we're saved by our mythopoeia. As soon as (for whatever reason) the tyrants fall or the foreigners leave – we leap up (like Karaghiozis with the Dragon[21]) and say: 'It was we who got rid of them!'

90 More myths: The Greeks as a 'chosen' people. The myth of Greek shrewdness. And the counter-myth of the gullible foreigner.

91 (Someday someone should write the strange romance between the xenophile and xenophobe in every Greek...)

92   Another myth: 'foreign intervention'. The modern
     Greeks have never been able to accept responsibility.
     Someone else was always to blame: those 'pulling
     the strings', the Intelligence Service, NATO, the
     CIA...

93   And this same myth also operates in our personal
     affairs: which candidate ever believes that he
     deserved to fail his exams? Which employee ever
     accepts that his colleague deserved promotion? The
     others always have 'the right connections'.

94   The myth of 'the right connections' is the opium that
     benumbs the sense of responsibility in the soul of
     the Greek.

95   Of course this is not to say that 'the right
     connections' and 'foreign interventions' are purely
     imaginary. All myths are based on reality. Yet the
     importance that all this intervening acquires in the
     ordinary Greek's imagination is truly metaphysical.

96   Another symptom: the constant demythologization
     of others and mythologization of ourselves. The
     total inability of the modern Greek to talk of any
     notable fellow Greek without qualifying: 'Yes,
     but...'

97   The comparison of everyone else with ourselves
     is compulsory. Necessary. The simple presence of

the other personally offends us. It threatens us. It has to be 'annulled'. The anxiety of constant competitiveness.

98 We are sometimes a small people with great ideas – and sometimes a great people with small ideas...

99 Is there any modern Greek, I wonder, whose manliness has never been questioned?

100 (At this point, we might recall the two most common Greek invectives...[22])

101 Another symptom in the absence of self-assurance: the modern Greek suspiciousness. The immediate reaction to whatever you say: 'Are you... kidding me?'

102 The Greek doesn't feel *comfortable* in the world. Like a relative from the provinces, he sits on the edge of his seat and conceals his lack of self-assurance behind his air of seriousness. He rarely laughs.

103 And yet laughter is perhaps the only proof of human freedom.

104 It is between myth and fear that the Greeks live and create.

Greek Reality (samples)

Institutions

105 Other peoples have institutions. We have mirror images.

106 The Greek 'establishment'! A pale, miserable imitation of an establishment. A paper tiger. The only thing saving it is that the Greek anti-establishment is in an even worse mess.

107 The only dangerous institutions in Greece are gerontocracy, bureaucracy and matriarchy.

108 'Bureaucracy is the illness for which it believes it is the cure.'[23]

109 Greeks continue to view their State as if it were a Turkish *vilayet*. They have every right to.

Economy

110 We shouldn't shout about Big Capital in Greece – because there is none. Fortunately, Big Capital still sees our country as a very small footnote.

111 Greek business basically consists of thirty or so large companies all dependent on one bank, which is controlled by the State.[24] (So you see, we also have socialism in Greece...)

112 It's not so much our capitalists who are exploiters of the Greeks' labor as the exponents of the glorious Greek tradition of spivs. Middle-men, agents, wheelers and dealers (Greek-American or not).

113 The classic Greek capitalist is still at the 'head of the family household' level.

114 The only major Greek capitalists are our shipowners – but they live outside Greece.

115 The worst form of capitalism is not personal (paternalistic, domestic), but rather impersonal.

116 Greek businesses are basically family enterprises. They retain all the warmth but also all the cruelty of the family atmosphere.

117 Modern Greek 'management'. Instead of motivation, a clout round the head from Karaghiozis.

118 The recent idyll between the Greeks and the consumer society – a long and bitter betrothal, with no marriage at the end.

Education

119 Greek education: a mechanism for the mass force-feeding of knowledge operated by uneducated, uncultured and underpaid instructors.

120 The problem with Greek education is a teacher problem. Only a personality can shape personalities. Behind every integrated person there is (always) at least one good teacher.

121 While ever the majority of teachers are who they are, education will be memorizing and not cultivation. Learning and not acumen.

122 I always remember the teachers who were terrified of those pupils who had learned how to think.

123 The principle on which Greek education was based was worse than non-existent. It was a contradiction in terms: *Greco-Christian* civilization. Two reciprocally rebutting concepts in one adjective. How characteristic of our inner paradox!

Religion

124 Other peoples have religion. We have Orthodox
papades – priests.

125 The only contact that the Greek Church has had with
anything spiritual in the last hundred years was the
excommunication of Roidis, Laskaratos[25] and
Kazantzakis.

126 In the last century, the Greek Church has – faithfully
and devotedly – served many masters. All except the
One.

Society

127 Statistical parameters concerning the average Greek (1975): he lives in the most expensive country in Europe – in relation to his salary – has the worst social insurance, the most road accidents, the poorest education system and the lowest book production. (I hope there might be found a country like Portugal to prove me wrong in some of the above.)

128 The worst thing that can be said about the Greek bourgeoisie is that it doesn't exist.

129 The Greek self-called 'aristocracy' are in reality the few real bourgeois – from well-to-do families. The nouveaux-bourgeois are in actual fact European-costumed (and bewildered) peasants. And the few remaining peasants are perhaps the only genuine Greeks.

130 The lack of any system in Greece prevented the proper development of even the class system.

131 The abruptly urbanized peasant is the saddest creature in Greece. His life has completely degenerated. He has lost all his traditional patriarchal background – without having acquired anything in its place. Nor did the Greek bourgeois

class have any tradition of note to offer him – and even if it had, a few thousand bourgeois couldn't possibly absorb a few million peasants in the space of one generation.

132 And so the urbanized peasant lives in a void. He has no land, no language (I'm coming 'by via Omonia Square', as even George Seferis wrote[26]), no religion. He no longer knows how to laugh or cry. Or how to live.

133 Nor even how to die. The most important criterion for the genuineness of a society is the way that it confronts death. In Greece, it's only in the villages that they still know how to face Charon.

134 If I had to choose the most characteristic symbol of modern Greek cheapness and vulgarity, I'd choose our ridiculous American hearses, with their kitsch crystal lamps. Never was something so serious more debased by its symbol.

Emigration

135 While half the Greeks were trying to transform Greece into a foreign country, the other half were emigrating.

136 We are one of the few countries that had more emigrants and refugees than inhabitants.

137 Greeks will always seek their homeland in other homelands – and other homelands in their own.

Kin

138 Just as a man is burdened by original sin – so a Greek is burdened by his kin.

139 In other countries people have relatives. In Greece they have associates in life (and death).

140 When a Greek doesn't have kin, he has his 'mates'.[27]

141 They are like his kin in that they are equally unchanging, equally demanding and equally boring.

142 (While ever the kin and the group of chums functioned in a proper social context, they were both genuine and positive. Now the essence has gone and only the convention has remained.)

Sex

143 The sexual life of Greek men moves on two levels: the real and the imaginary. The distance between them is great.

144 The sexual life of Greek women also moves on two levels: the real and the commercial. The distance between them is small.

145 The most ingenious entrepreneurial ideas of the Greek tycoons pale before the daily sex-trade activity of the average Greek female.

146 The exploitation of women by men has as its natural consequence the deception of men by women.

147 However, it is the woman-mother who has the final word. Here, using the most subtle weapons (overpowering 'love' and 'guilt'), she takes her revenge. By creating children-slaves or children-revolutionaries.

148 Whereas a Greek man has to struggle to break free of himself, the Greek woman has to wage war to break free of the Greek man. The time for her to struggle with herself comes later.

Environment

149 All the method and system missing from our everyday lives and work is concentrated in our secret mission: to destroy as effectively as we can this lovely land allotted to us by fate.

150 The truth is that this land is so beautiful that at times its beauty weighs upon our souls, rather like the shadow of our ancestors. Yet another Greek complex.

151 Somewhere inside us we believe that we don't deserve to live in such a lovely land. And we try to bring it into line with 'our own standards'. Our own level. So we cover it with concrete and refuse.

152 Greece never ever dies![28] (Don't give up hope: Let's all keep trying...)

153 The Greek landscape: something between Poussin's *Les Bergers d'Arcadie* and the Theatre of the Absurd. Today: scenery for tourists.

154 Whatever was fashioned by nature and the ancient Greeks... (Now become one and the same.) And we, a motley troupe, wander about amid a splendid scenery for tragedy.

155 Searching backstage, behind the scenery, for the true face of your land, you discover in terror that it's not stage-scenery but actual stone and rock. You're the only thing that's fake. An actor. A ham!

156 'Wherever I travel, Greece wounds me.'[29]

157 Put Greece in your heart and you'll suffer cardiac arrest.[30]

Intellect

158 The most piteous thing in the world: ten Greek intellectuals in one room. Each of them trying to make an audience of the others.

159 An intellectual is someone who tries (usually in vain) to put his ideas into practice. A Greek intellectual is someone who tries to find ideas in order to justify what he practices.

160 Intellectual communication in Greece: periodically and consecutively, the transmitters are transformed into receivers so as to congratulate other trans-mitters (without having read them), so that they too may be eventually transformed into transmitters, etc. Intellectual incest...

161 If you go to a concert, an exhibition, a lecture, you've seen them all. That's them. A thousand? Probably fewer. A closed (vicious) circle of the intellect.

162 Greece is probably the only country where the author pays out of his own pocket to get a book published and then is taxed on 'income from authorship rights'.

163 The hard-sell by which the promotion of intellectual values takes place in the west is a thousand times

preferable to the smarminess, baseness and favoritism that characterize intellectual life in Greece.

164 (All those members of the National Literary Awards committee who have reached this far in the book deserve praise for their conscientiousness and their diligence...)

165 Better a coolie in olden-day China than an intellectual in Greece.

166 If the intellectuals and artists are the unhappiest people (because with them the gap between desire and reality acquires tragic proportions)...
And if the Greeks are the unhappiest of all peoples...
Then what could be worse than being a Greek intellectual?

Epilogue

167 Let the Greek soul be whatever it will – all except one thing: cheap and anonymous.

168 This is the great danger. So 'resist!' as the poet said.[31] But resist in Greek fashion.

169 And the Greek hyperbole and complexes and uncertainty lead to creativity. It's sleep and lethargy and that sated 'couldn't care less' that you should be afraid of.

170 The Greeks, consumers of happiness… Karaghiozis' constant dream! But how painful on waking up.

171 Perhaps because the true happiness of the Greek is not the static equilibrium (always temporary anyway) between demand and supply, but life's dialectic of struggle.

172 We Greeks must be mad. Just as, for the bourgeois, the tragic hero is mad. A 'great holy madness'[32] is the only true thing we have achieved up to now – whether it succeeded or not.

173 Which is why many liked the struggle itself more than the goal of the struggle.

174 We all seek happiness. Yet if people ever succeed in becoming completely reconciled with reality, the – tragic and struggling – Greek spirit will have been lost.

175 Reconciliation with reality means either the (momentary) overcoming or ignorance of reality. Benumbing and forgetting. But the limits always exist. Inexorably.

176 'And what about death, comrade?'[33] Indeed, comrades, peoples of the world, what about death?

177 For three thousand years, the Greeks have worshipped life. From Homer to Elytis.[34]

178 'To live and gaze upon the sun's light'.[35]

179 No promise of any future life could ever compensate a Greek for the loss of the earthly paradise. No religion could ever reconcile him with death... His transcendentalism was always within this world. Only the 'now' has the value of 'forever'.

180 The ultimate Greek tragedy: to love life more than you can bear. Greek hyperbole in its most extreme form. And the extreme unhappiness of the Greek.

181 Greek pessimism is created by an excessive affirmation of life and not by its renunciation. By the inability to reconcile yourself with life's finiteness.

182 All those who loved this land died young, either suicides or mad.

183 Greece is a cruel mistress.

184 Will this people ever find its face? Or is its true face a contradiction?

185 The face of Greece: 'of which so many aspects are apparent and so many are concealed'.[36] Better so. Because, perhaps, it would be impossible to gaze upon it entirely. The light would dazzle you. The 'angelic and black light'.[37]

186 The Greek light. A great respite and a deadly weapon. ('In the shining light...destroy us.'[38]) Few dare to look at it. (And for this reason, always so many obscurantists in this country.)

187 All harsh shadow and light, this land. And our souls, too, harsh shadow and light. Dissenting and opposing.

188 A Greek: a strange, absurd, tragic moment in the history of humanity.

189 As God is my witness: nothing have I loved more than this land.

Postscript

190 Of course, one could also write a book entitled: *On the Happiness of Being Greek.*

191 Because this happiness exists (who would dare to deny it?).

192 So there you are: in writing about unhappiness, I've also been writing about happiness.

193 About the happiness of the unhappiness of being Greek.

Athens 1975

Postscript 2012

People who enjoy reading this book are probably not Greek. For a Greek this book is painful. He may smile at some aphorisms, even laugh sometimes, but closing it, he will feel, well... unhappy. It portrays the basic problem of his existence, his urge for more and his inability to cope with less. Conflicts undermine his identity, make him uncertain and changeable. He is divided between his glorious past and his meager present, between his Eastern mentality and his European aspiration – torn asunder by forces of tradition (like the Orthodox Church) and modernity. His is a difficult fate.

This book is not a humorous collection of aphorisms about the shortcomings of Greeks – but a bitter reflection on their tragic destiny of being split among past and present, north and south, east and west. It is a declaration of love for Greece, the true, the profound Greece – and not the superficial land of myths that Greek themselves have created in order to escape from reality. By no means is it the work of an 'Anti-Hellene' but the product of a man who cares deeply for his country, and tries to help his fellow citizens fulfill the Delphic motto: 'Know thyself.' Something that can be a painful procedure, if your mentality, education and upbringing have taught you to avoid truth.

Greece's present predicament is to a large extend the result of all these flaws in the national character. More emotional and less rational, a Greek must re-think himself in order to survive in the modern world. This book tries to help him on the way.

N. D.

Notes

1. Emmanuel Roides (1836–1904). Greek author, literary critic and essayist. Best known for his satirical novel *Pope Joan*.
2. Quoted from Dionysios Solomos (1798–1857), who is regarded as the national poet of Modern Greece.
3. Theodoros Kolokotronis (1770–1843). Hero of the Greek War of Independence.
4. Karaghiozis. Comic puppet character from the Greek popular shadow theater. Embodiment of all the virtues and failings of the modern Greek. By extension someone who provokes ridicule.
5. Edmond About (1828–1885). Author of *Le Roi des Montagnes*.
6. Lit. 'love of honor'. A strong (often excessive) sense of personal honor and self-respect.
7. No exact equivalent term in English. A person exhibiting dash, valor, uprightness, pride, etc.
8. Grumbling, but also constant complaining, griping, moaning, negativity, etc.
9. Another character from the Greek popular shadow theater. He forever plays the poor and suffering wretch, but is only ever interested in personal gain.
10. From the poem entitled 'Mycenae' by the Greek poet George Seferis (1900–1971). Nobel Prize for Literature 1963.
11. General Makriyannis (1797–1864). Hero of the Greek War of Independence. Unlettered, he taught

himself to write in order to record his memoirs of the War.

12. Theophilos Hadjimichail (1870–1934). Naïf painter from Lesbos.

13. Jakob Philipp Fallmerayer (1790–1861). German historian who claimed that the Slavs who overran Greece in the 6th and 7th centuries so changed the ethnic character of the country that not a drop of pure Hellenic blood was left.

14. Oscar Wilde, Preface to *The Picture of Dorian Gray*.

15. The quotation is from Emmanuel Roides.

16. Count Ioannis Antonios Capodistrias (1776–1832). First president of Greece. He was assassinated.

17. In 1833, Otto of Bavaria became the first King of Greece following the War of Independence.

18. Indigenous and Orthodox Albanian-speaking communities.

19. From a well-known verse by the poet Andreas Kalvos (1792–1869).

20. Traditional and patriotic saying.

21. Well-known story involving Karaghiozis. The dragon plaguing the town is killed by Alexander the Great. Finding the dragon slain and in order to claim the reward, Karaghiozis pretends that it was he who slew it.

22. Namely: *malakas* (wanker) and *poustis* (poofter).

23. Variation on the well-known aphorism of the Austrian Carl Krauss.

24. As was the case when the book was first published in 1975.

25. Andreas Laskaratos (1811–1901). Excommunicated after publishing the prose satire *The Mysteries of Cephallonia* (1856).
26. See the poem 'In the Manner of G. S.'.
27. Greek *parea*. No exact cultural equivalent in English in the sense used here. A group of close friends who spend their time together. People bonded by companionship.
28. Patriotic Greek march.
29. George Seferis. See the poem 'In the Manner of G. S.'.
30. Variation on a well-known phrase from Dionyios Solomos: 'Put Greece in your heart and you'll feel every kind of greatness.'
31. Michalis Katsaros (1919–1998). Greek poet. Reference to his well-known poem entitled 'Resist'.
32. Reference to a line by the poet Angelos Sikelianos (1884–1951).
33. The author notes that this was the only question left unanswered by André Malraux at a pre-War conference of the French Communist Party.
34. Odysseus Elytis (1911–1996). Greek poet. Nobel Prize for Literature 1979.
35. Formula found often in Homer's *Iliad* to characterize someone living.
36. Dionysios Solomos. 'The Free Besieged', Draft III.
37. Reference to a line by George Seferis.
38. Homer, *Iliad*, Rhapsody R, 647.

Contemporary culture has eliminated both the concept of the public and the figure of the intellectual. Former public spaces – both physical and cultural – are now either derelict or colonized by advertising. A cretinous anti-intellectualism presides, cheerled by expensively educated hacks in the pay of multinational corporations who reassure their bored readers that there is no need to rouse themselves from their interpassive stupor. The informal censorship internalized and propagated by the cultural workers of late capitalism generates a banal conformity that the propaganda chiefs of Stalinism could only ever have dreamt of imposing. Zer0 Books knows that another kind of discourse – intellectual without being academic, popular without being populist – is not only possible: it is already flourishing, in the regions beyond the striplit malls of so-called mass media and the neurotically bureaucratic halls of the academy. Zer0 is committed to the idea of publishing as a making public of the intellectual. It is convinced that in the unthinking, blandly consensual culture in which we live, critical and engaged theoretical reflection is more important than ever before.